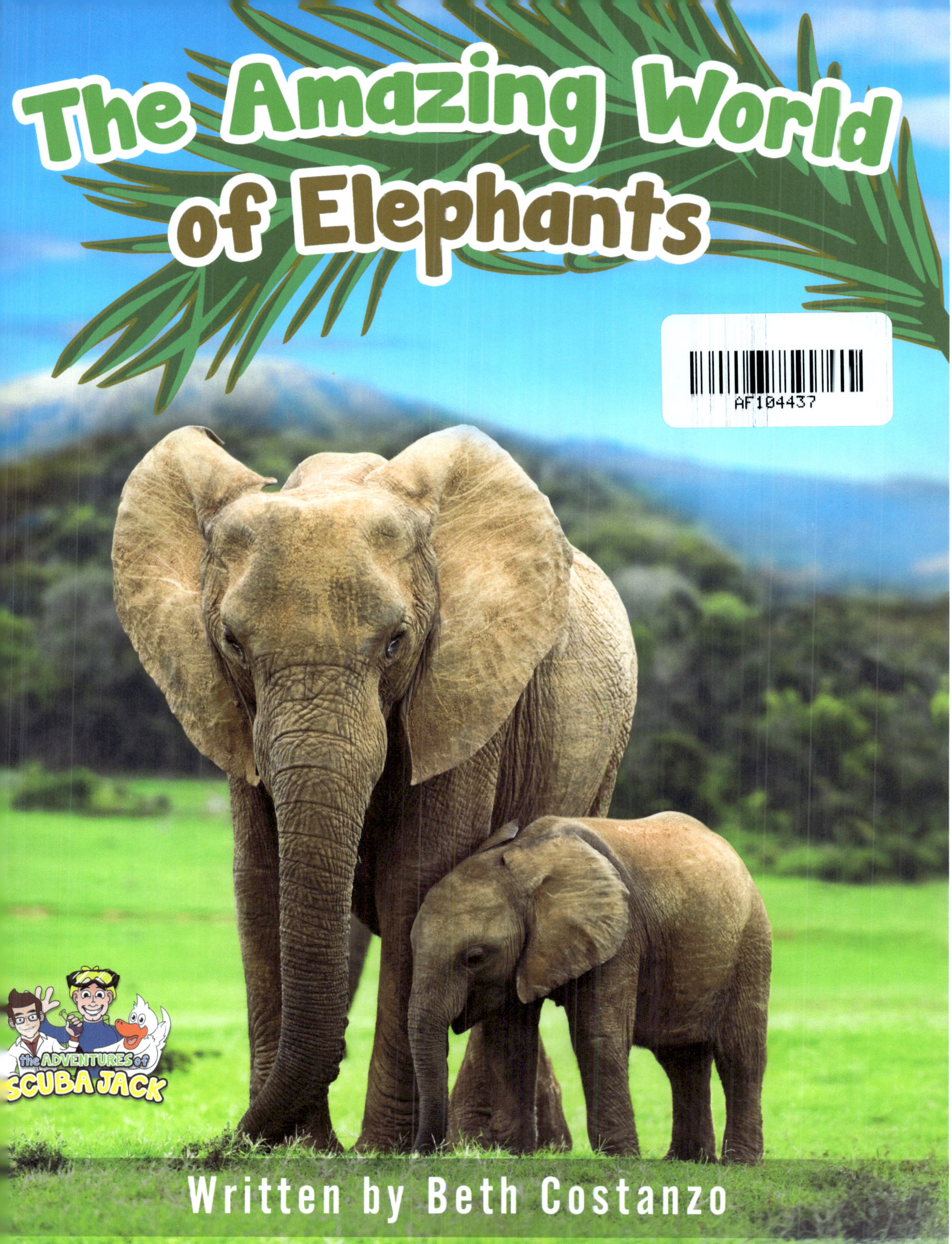

Copyright 2020 - by Beth Costanzo

Elephants are some of the most fascinating creatures in our animal kingdom. You have probably seen them in your local zoo or on television. They are large, lumbering animals who famously "never forget." In fact, they are the largest existing land animals, so you'll want to stay out of their way if you find them in the wild!

Ultimately, there are plenty of fun and interesting facts about elephants. Whether you are speaking with friends, family, or classmates, you can use these facts to show how much you know about one of the most interesting mammals on Earth today.

The Elephant: One of Earth's Most Enchanting Creatures

Any discussion about elephants starts with its size. Like we said above, elephants are the largest land animals on our planet. The largest species of elephants (called the African bush elephant) is around 10 to 11 feet tall (for males) and 8 to 9 feet tall (for females). Even the smallest species of elephants (called the African forest elephant) is quite large, as it is around seven feet tall. Along with its large height, the elephant is an extremely heavy animal. The largest African bush elephants weigh about 7 tons, which is 14,000 pounds.

www.adventuresofscubajack.com

Along with their size, it's hard not to notice the elephant's ears, feet, long trunk, and tusks. Its trunk, for instance, has many functions, including breathing, smelling, touching, and grasping. Its tusks are actually teeth and grow continuously at around 7 inches per ear. It uses its tusks to do things like peel off tree bark that it can later eat.

www.adventuresofscubajack.com

To put it simply, elephants are huge. From that, you would think that the elephant's huge size makes it one of the slowest creatures on our planet. Surprisingly, elephants can travel quickly. They can reach a top speed of around sixteen miles per hour, meaning that they can outrun many humans. You don't want to be in their way when they are charging!

From the physical characteristics of elephants, let's move on to where you can find elephants in the wild. While you may be able to see them in your local zoo, wild elephants are located in Africa and Asia. They are found in habitats like savannahs, deserts, marshes, and forests. For reasons including poaching and habitat destruction, African and Asian elephants are considered to be vulnerable species. No matter where you see elephants in the wild, you can be sure that people are working hard to make sure that they do not go extinct.

In terms of their food, elephants are herbivores. This means that elephants only eat plants. Along with plants, elephants tend to eat twigs, fruit, bark, roots, and grass. They often coexist peacefully with other herbivores. They aren't fighting with them over their food and will usually stay out of other herbivores' way. Per day, elephants can consume about 330 pounds of food and 11 gallons of water per day. This is a huge amount of food, requiring the elephant to feed in the morning, afternoon, and at night.

Beyond food, elephants are extremely intelligent animals. They have a trait called mirror self-recognition, which basically means that they have higher awareness and thinking compared to other animals. Elephants are one of the few species that have been known to use tools. And like we said at the beginning, elephants are known to have great memories. Individual elephants can even keep track of where their family members currently are.

Elephants communicate with each other by touching. They can even greet each other by wrapping or stroking their huge trunks. If elephants feel threatened in a particular situation, they will raise their heads and spread their ears. If they are especially excited, they will raise their trunks. Elephants can sometimes be aggressive and attack humans and villages, but this is rare.

Dangers To Elephants

Elephants typically do not threaten other animals. This is because they are herbivores. Truthfully, the biggest threat to elephants is not from other animals, but from humans. The poaching of elephants for their ivory is one of the major threats to their existence. While there are poaching bans in many African countries, elephants continue to be threatened by humans who are looking to make money from their bodies.

Finally, we can't talk about elephants without talking about baby elephants. Besides being extremely cute, baby elephants are fascinating. They are born during the wet season and are born at around 33 inches tall and weigh 260 pounds. Newborn elephants quickly learn to stand and follow their mothers. Yes, the newborn elephant is unsteady on its feet for the first few days, but it quickly stabilizes. For the first three months, it relies on its mother's milk for nutrition. After that, it begins eating plants and using its trunk to drink water.

www.adventuresofscubajack.com

Some More Fun Facts About Elephants

www.adventuresofscubajack.com

As you can tell, elephants are simply fascinating. But luckily, the facts don't stop there. Here you will find some additional fun facts about elephants that you can share with all of your friends.

- Elephants produce several sounds. The most well-known sound is the trumpet sound that is made by elephants blowing through their trunks.

- Elephants have worked with humans throughout history. For example, they have been used to haul equipment into remote areas and transport tourists around national parks. Elephants have even been used as instruments of war.

- Male elephants looking to breed participate in a practice called mate-guarding. Basically, this means that male elephants follow certain females and defend them from other male elephants. Doing this, male elephants are more likely to have children.

- Elephants have about 326 to 351 bones. They also have 26 teeth.

- Elephant skin is very thick. It can be one inch thick on its back and parts of its head.

- Scientists debate whether elephants feel emotion. Some have found that dying or dead elephants lead to attention and concern from others.

- An elephant's trunk can lift up to 770 pounds.

- Elephants in many cultures represent positive traits like power, wisdom, strength, and leadership.

Elephants Activities

www.adventuresofscubajack.com

TRACING

Trace the word then write it

Elephant

www.adventuresofscubajack.com

MAZE

Help the baby elephant to find his mom

www.adventuresofscubajack.com

COUNTING

Circle the correct answer

4 6 5	6 7 5
4 5 3	7 8 6

www.adventuresofscubajack.com

COLORING

www.adventuresofscubajack.com

Visit us at:

www.adventuresofscubajack.com